Understanding "Uncle Tom's Cabin" and "The Battle Hymn of the Republic":

How Novelist Harriet Beecher Stowe and Poet Julia Ward Howe Influenced the Northern Mind

Historical Studies by Howard Ray White

First I should express appreciation to the National Portrait Gallery in Washington, DC for the photographs of the paintings on the cover. The upper image is of Julia Ward Howe and the lower is of Harriet Beecher Stowe.

The **most influential literary contribution** to the politics of the northern States during the mid-to-late 1850's — helping incite State Secession and a horrific four-year war that killed 360,000 Federals — was Harriet Beecher Stowe's novel, *"Uncle Tom's Cabin,"* published in 1851-52, just before the onset of "Bleeding Kansas."

Likewise, that war's **most influential music/poetry contribution** — morally justifying, in the minds of many northern States people, the military conquest of the Confederacy and the huge death toll suffered — was Julia Ward Howe's poem, *"The Battle Hymn of the Republic"* (1861), a variation upon the then-recent Federal army camp folk song, *"John Brown's Body,"* which was an intentional mockery of a very popular, traditional South Carolina church revival song, *"Say, Brothers,"* its music and lyrics written by William Steffe a few years earlier. The *"Battle Hymn"* is handed down to us today as "lyrics by Julia Ward Howe and music by William Steffe."

The two essays in this booklet are excerpted from Howard Ray White's four volume history, titled, *"Bloodstains, an Epic History of the Politics that Produced and Sustained the American Civil War and the Political Reconstruction that Followed."* This booklet and other works by the writer are available as e-books and as paper books on Amazon.com. Search "Howard Ray White".

In the mid-1800's women were not to be leaders in politics and religion, but Harriet Beecher Stowe and Julia Ward Howe did just that. Of Harriet, daughter of Lyman Beecher and sister of Henry Ward Beecher, both influential Abolitionists/ministers/educators, Sinclair Lewis would write: *"Uncle Tom's Cabin* was the first

1

evidence to America that no hurricane can be so disastrous to a country as a ruthlessly humanitarian woman." The same could be equally said of Julia, a close friend of Charles Sumner and, wife of Boston Abolitionist leader Samuel Howe, one of the "Secret Six" financial supporters of the notorious John Brown.

White's other books include:

- ***Bloodstains, An Epic History of the Politics that Produced and Sustained the American Civil War and the Political Reconstruction that Followed***, presented in 4 volumes — Volume 1, ***The Nation Builders***; Volume 2, ***The Demagogues***; Volume 3, ***The Bleeding***, and Volume 4, ***Political Reconstruction and the Struggle for Healing***.

- ***Understanding Abe Lincoln's First Shot Strategy*** *(Inciting the First Shot at Fort Sumter)*.

- ***Advancing American Reading Achievement during the Great Depression*** (by L. J. Willis, edited by Howard Ray White).

- ***Understanding Creation and Evolution: A Biblical and Scientific Comparative Study***.

- ***Springfield Girl, a Memoir*** (by Martha Frances Bell White, edited by Howard Ray White).

- ***Understanding Granddad through His Poetry*** (poems by John Andrew White, edited by Howard Ray White).

Table of Contents

Understanding "Uncle Tom's Cabin."

Introduction.

One's understanding of American political history is incomplete until he or she has factually studied the novel that unquestionably exerted the greatest literary influence on the emotional political controversy that erupted in the horrific War Between the States. I am speaking of course of the 1852 novel, *Uncle Tom's Cabin*, by Harriet Beecher Stowe, daughter of the famous Congregational minister, Lyman Beecher and sister to an equally famous preacher, Henry Ward Beecher. Of the thousands of books and magazine articles, and of the tens of thousands of newspaper stories, that accused the people of the southern States of inhumane treatment of bonded African Americans (slaves), Stowe's *Uncle Tom's Cabin* was the most influential. It was a propaganda masterpiece that became bigger than life and painted for many northern States people their mistaken perception of the people of the southern States – a people of a different culture living far away to their south, who very, very few would visit, save as a soldier in an invading army. I remember my mother reading sections of the novel to me as a child. I would ask her to read to be about "Topsy."

If you merely quickly read the complete novel, *Uncle Tom's Cabin*, as published, there will be much you will not understand sufficiently to factually evaluate its historical impact upon the diverse 1850's American psychic in the northern States. Therefore, to speed your understanding of the novel and its impact, I have prepared for you an efficient alternative. What follows below is a condensed version of the novel, presented in terminology you will find especially helpful. This brief booklet concludes with related biography and the history surrounding the novel and its creation.

I need to define a few terms that I have adopted to help my understanding, and I hope yours as well. You will observe that I speak of "bonded African Americans" instead of "slaves." I do this to focus on the fact that, with few exceptions, those being illegal, a person of less than one-eight African racial ancestry could not be held in bondage to another person (as his or her slave). I will also keep you informed about the racial ancestry of characters in Stowe's novel, because she was far more concerned about holding in bondage a person of one-forth to one-eighth African racial ancestry, as opposed to a person of one half to full African racial ancestry, meaning that

4

her novel mostly featured characters with skin and hair that more nearly resembled that of European Americans.

I also divide the Anti-Slavery Movement into its three distinctly different advocacies, as follows:

First, there were **Abolitionists**, who, if true to their name, advocated making bonded African Americans independent (free or emancipated) and permitting them to live and work anywhere in the American States, including in their towns as their neighbors — for example, with folks in Illinois. Abolitionists of this unbiased and humane philosophy were few and far between, numbering about two percent of the population of the northern States. Furthermore, Abolitionists never organized a charity aimed at buying bonded African Americans and helping them transition to independent life in America; almost all Abolitionists remained content to merely condemn slavery, to feel morally superior for doing so.

Second, there were the **Deportationists**, who advocated making bonded African Americans independent just prior deporting them out of the American States, to perhaps Africa (Liberia), the Caribbean Islands (Haiti) or Central or South America. Deportationists advocated the agenda of the American Colonization Society, which the famous Henry Clay led for a time. Furthermore, during the first year of the War Between the States, President Lincoln advocated Deportation and launched a trial Federal Deportation Program to Haiti. Unlike the Abolition Movement, Deportationism avoided permitting formerly bonded African Americans and their descendants from living and working anywhere in the American States. Deportationism was widely envisioned in the northern States as the "final solution."

Third, there were the **Exclusionists**, who advocated denying bonded African Americans the right to live outside of their homelands in the southern States. By this advocacy, bonded African Americans were excluded from the vast territories conquered from Mexico in 1848, which lay to the west of the established States, all the way to the Pacific Ocean. Exclusionism was the "immediate solution," and insistence on that policy by northern States voters, who represented the majority during the 1950's, eventually drove 7 southern States to secede in the winter of 1860-1861. A popular theory of the time, which sounds like non-sense to us today, held that Exclusionism would eventually lead to Deportation, thereby avoiding the societal consequences of Abolitionism. More on Harriet Beecher Stowe and her novel follows.

During 1851 Harriet Beecher Stowe wrote *Uncle Tom's Cabin* for serial publication in *The National Era*. After the magazine published the last episode, the work was published as a book, the first press run going on sale in March 1852. The novel would sell over 300,000 copies in one year alone. The work would be translated into 40 languages. The author and heirs would record 3,000,000 to 4,000,000 copies sold in America, over 1,500,000 sold in Great Britain, and 4,000,000 sold in foreign languages. Playwrights would be free to create dramatic plays without paying copyright fees and these would be popular, particularly George Aiken's interpretation that would open in New York City in the winter of 1853. *Uncle Tom's Cabin*, essentially a novel, would be by far the most influential Abolitionist and Exclusionist propaganda publication to ever influence the American mind. Historians would later conclude that *Uncle Tom's Cabin* was a significant contributor to the rise of sectional hatred and the disintegration, within the Federation of sovereign States (collectively known as the United States), of normal bonds of brotherhood. Abolitionists and Exclusionists would acclaim the novel and its author and credit both for major contributions toward the triumph of northern States political sectionalism.

You may wonder what Abe Lincoln was doing during the early 1850's. Well, except for one brief speaking tour in Massachusetts, he was, at that time, limiting his horizon to central Illinois, making good money as a trial lawyer. He would have little interest in Abolition and Exclusion Activism until 1856. So he was not involved in early 1850's propaganda and, in fact, would first meet Harriet Beecher Stowe when she would visit him at the White House in 1862. At that time Lincoln would greet the literary idol with these telling words: "So this is the little lady who made this big war?"

It is fitting to now summarize, condense, the novel, *Uncle Tom's Cabin*.

"Uncle Tom's Cabin," a Condensation.

Uncle Tom is a bonded African American who lives and works on a farm within a day's walk of the Ohio River in northern Kentucky,

perhaps no more than 30 miles from Cincinnati. He and his wife Chloe have 2 small children. Tom is a devout Christian who loves to read his *Bible* and hold prayer meetings. He is an exceptionally honest, trustworthy and good man. He is strong and healthy, but his owner, Mr. Shelby, primarily relies on Tom to help manage the farm. Mr. and Mrs. Shelby, long-time Kentuckians, treat their bonded servants well. Horses seem to be the main product of the farm. Tom is primarily, perhaps totally, of African descent. Chloe, who is of similar ancestry, is the cook and an excellent one at that. Tom and Chloe live in a private cabin on the farm with their children. Eliza also lives and works on the farm. The personal servant of the farmer's wife, she lives in a small room in the main house with her young son Harry. Eliza is married to a young man named George who lives on a farm several miles away. Eliza, George and little Harry are bonded, but their ancestry is at least three-fourth's European, for their coloration is so light that people in passing sometimes mistake them for European Americans.

The story begins with Mr. Shelby in unfortunate financial debt to a slave trader who insists that he must take and resell Uncle Tom and little Harry in settlement of the obligation. The trader refuses to accept any substitutes for Tom or little Harry for reasons that are never explained. Mr. and Mrs. Shelby hate to part with either because Tom is married with two children and is so important to the success for the farm, and because little Harry is far too young to leave his parents. We are led to believe that the farm might fall into bankruptcy if the trade is refused. Tom, a heart of gold, agrees to cooperate if it means that the farm will survive and remain a home for all the rest, and apparently Mr. Shelby agrees to make the sale. However, a few hours after the sell is finalized, but before the trader takes possession, Eliza runs away with little Harry to keep the trader from taking her son. There is a chase, but Eliza manages to heroically cross the Ohio River by leaping from ice flow to ice flow until she reaches the Ohio side. Eliza and Harry immediately receive help from an Ohio State Senator who lives beside the river. The Senator takes the pair to a compassionate farmer where they stay for a while. A day or two later, Eliza's husband George runs away from his owner, a hateful man who beats George because he is jealous that George is the more intelligent and capable man. We are told that George's father was a very intelligent and successful European American and the father had passed on to the son a substantial dose of these admirable traits. A faithful husband, George will be looking for Eliza and Harry so they can be reunited.

Meanwhile the trader consummates the purchase of Uncle Tom. He takes Tom to an estate sale where he buys additional bonded African Americans, including a young boy, of perhaps 12, who sadly is forced to leave his mother. The trader then boards a riverboat with his people and travels down river towards Louisville. Further down the river the trader debarks and returns with a young bonded African American woman and her nursing baby. Although it seems illogical, we are told that there is a man on the boat who, seeing the pair, wants to purchase only the nursing baby and we are told that the trader agrees to the sale because his prospective customer in New Orleans would not want a woman with a baby. Again a trade separates a child from its mother. The next night the mother commits suicide by leaping overboard into the frigid water. The riverboat enters the Mississippi River and moves south toward New Orleans.

Shortly before reaching New Orleans a little girl named Eva falls off the boat into the river just as the paddle wheels began turning. Both the girl's father and Uncle Tom see the accident, but Tom is first into the river after her. He quickly grabs her and lifts her up to fellow passengers. The little girl had enjoyed playing with Uncle Tom during the long boat ride, and, acceding to her wishes, her father, Augustine St. Clare, agrees to purchase Uncle Tom to work about his spacious New Orleans house.

Augustine St. Clare's father had moved to Louisiana from Canada many years before and made a fortune with a large cotton farm. Augustine had been raised on that farm, but detested farm life and preferred to let his brother run the inherited family business while he remained in town. The St. Clare town house is immense. It seems to spill over with many more servants than the workload justified. Uncle Tom is given quarters over the carriage house and made responsible for driving the carriage, but he has an assistant who grooms the horses for him. It appears that Augustine's hobby is collecting bonded African Americans because he wants to take care of them. Although she should have been in the prime of life, Augustine's wife, Marie is sickly and lays around the house all day complaining of weakness and headaches. She seems to care only about her aches and pains. Augustine has no job to go to, nor a sport he likes to play. Augustine and his daughter had been returning by riverboat from visiting relatives in Vermont, and had brought back with him his spinster cousin, Miss Ophelia, who planned a long, long visit in New Orleans.

Unlike Tom, many of the bonded African American house servants are predominantly of European descent, and they feel a sense of superiority toward African Americans outside the house, because most outsiders are of pure or nearly pure African descent. Augustine and Miss Ophelia discuss the rights and wrongs of African American bonding at great length. Marie complains that she is a slave herself – to the obligation to keep up so many servants. Augustine obviously spends a lot of money in support of his over-staffed household. Mammy, another bonded servant who works as Eva's nanny, is mostly of European descent and extremely loving toward the child – in sharp contrast to the coldness of the child's natural mother. Eva enjoys playing with Uncle Tom and the two develop a loving companionship. Tom remains a dedicated Christian. His primary job seems to be evangelizing the household, especially Augustine and little Eva.

The story returns north to Ohio and George, Eliza and little Harry. George has found his wife and son in the care of a Quaker community. But, soon after the reunion, they are forced to flee from a pair of catchers hired by the slave-trader who had paid Mr. Shelby for Harry before Eliza and the child had run away. Two Quakers take them (and a run-away named Jim and his mother) toward Canada in a wagon, but they are about to be overtaken by the catchers, they jump from the wagon and take refuge in a massive rock outcropping, which provides excellent defense. As the two catchers and their helpers ponder how to best capture them, George mounts a prominent rock and declares their independence with poetic exhilaration:

"You mean to take my wife to sell in New Orleans, and put my boy like a calf in a trader's pen, and send Jim's old mother to the brute that whipped and abused her before, because he could not abuse her son. You want to send Jim and me back to be whipped and tortured, and ground down under the heels of them that you call masters; and your laws *will* bear you out in it – more shame for you and them! But you have not got us. We don't own your laws; we don't own your country; we stand here as free, under God's sky, as you are; and, by the great God that made us, we'll fight for our liberty till we die."

George's speech is answered with a bullet from the unsympathetic catcher's gun that barely misses its mark. George immediately resumes his defensive position in the rocks. Then a catcher named Loker decides to brave the defense and charges in after George only to be shot in the side by one of George's two fine pistols. Loker falls wounded to the base of the rocks. The others are less brave and ride off. The Quakers and George put Loker in the wagon and take him to a Quaker friend who nurses him to health. We are told that Loker is converted to Christianity and thereafter leads an honorable life. George, Eliza and little Harry make it to Canada, drawing no notice at the border crossing since they look so European.

Back in New Orleans Miss Ophelia undertakes the unnecessary task of teaching the underemployed household servants her brand of Vermont-style, hard-working efficiency. She starts with the kitchen servants and the head cook, Dinah. Although disorganized and messy, Dinah is putting splendid meals on the table. Miss Ophelia's concern is the efficiency of Dinah's methods, not her results. But the St. Clare household consists of more servants, money and time than any of them know what to do with; consequently Miss Ophelia is trying to apply a solution where there is no real problem. The cook remains inefficient but effective. Miss Ophelia complains to Augustine that Dinah refuses to be taught efficiency, but he shrugs the problem off with:

> "My dear Vermont, you natives up by the North Pole set an extravagant value on time! What on earth is the use of time to a fellow who has twice as much of it as he knows what to do with?"

An old woman named Prue makes a brief appearance in the story as a door-to-door bread seller. Prue is an elderly bonded African American who has been abused and whipped. She has taken to heavy drinking and suffered more whippings for her drunkenness. We are told Prue died from a final abusive whipping soon after her last visit to the St. Claire house. Such evil makes a big impression on little Eva. Miss Ophelia and Augustine continue their running debate over the right and wrong of African American bonding. Augustine explains how, many years earlier, his father had built a prosperous farm where 500 bonded African Americans had lived and worked, and that, after his father had died, he and his brother Alf had jointly run the business for a while, but eventually had agreed to part:

> "Alf and I came to about the same point that I and my respected father did, years before. So he told me that I was a womanish sentimentalist, and would never do for business life; and advised

me to take the bank-stock and the New Orleans family mansion, and go to writing poetry, and let him manage the [farm]. So we parted, and I came here."

Finally, Uncle Tom, after perhaps a year or two, arranges for Augustine to write a letter to his wife in Kentucky. Although he could read, Tom's writing skills and knowledge about addressing and sending letters was apparently insufficient. We can only wonder why Tom did not send more letters, and send them sooner.

We are next introduced to "Topsy," who is Harriet Stowe's only noteworthy literary achievement. Augustine says he has just purchased Topsy from "a couple of drunken creatures that keep a low restaurant that I have to pass by every day" because he "was tired of hearing her screaming, and them beating and swearing at her." Topsy, a lively little girl of 8 or 9, is of pure African descent, in sharp contrast to the house servants whose descent probably averages at least 50 percent European. Miss Ophelia asks, "Augustine, what in the world have you brought that thing here for?" He answers, "For you to educate, to be sure, and train in the way she should go." Topsy knows nothing of her mother and father. When Miss Ophelia asks the child, "Do you know who made you," Topsy replies with her most famous line: "I spect I grow'd. Don't think nobody never made me." At this point a servant explains, "Laws, Missis, there's heaps of 'em. Speculators buys 'em up cheap, when they's little, and gets 'em raised for market." Thus begins Miss Ophelia's comical efforts to train little Topsy to behave, to perform household chores, to read and write and to learn about God. The going is very slow, not because Topsy is slow of mind, but because she is too rambunctious and mischievous to behave herself and pay attention during instruction. Topsy becomes the focus of more discussion between Miss Ophelia and Augustine over the rights and wrongs of African American bonding. Miss Ophelia, who remains repulsed by Topsy's pure African appearance, tells Augustine, "I know I'd never let a child of mine play with Topsy." To this Augustine, who had lived with and played with African American children throughout his childhood, says, "Well, your children need not, but mine may; if Eva could have been spoiled, it would have been done years ago." A bit later Miss Ophelia complains, "I don't see how I'm going to manage that child, without whipping her." Augustine replies, "Well, whip her, then, to your heart's content; I'll give you full power to do what you like." Miss Ophelia answers, "Children always have to be whipped. I never heard of bringing them up without." When Miss Ophelia threatens to whip Topsy over misbehaving, the little girl responds, "Law, Missis, you must whip me; my old Missis allers whipped me. I an't used to workin' unless I gets whipped. . . . I's used to whippin'; I spects it's good for me." Then Miss Ophelia proceeds to give a light whipping to which Topsy responds with appropriate screaming and hollering. A bit later Topsy tells whoever might be listening, "Law, Miss Feely whip! – would n't kill a skeeter, her whippin's. Oughter see how old Mas'r made the flesh fly; old Mas'r know'd how!" Topsy seemed to thrive on believing herself a bad girl: "I spects I's the wickedest crittur in the world."

At this point the scene shifts to Kentucky where Uncle Tom's wife, Aunt Chloe, talks the Shelby's into letting her relocate to Louisville for a few years to earn money as a cook at a bakery. Chloe hopes to use the money to buy her husband back from the St Clare's. This arrangement had been prompted by receipt of the letter Augustine had written for Uncle Tom.

During the third or fourth year of Uncle Tom's stay in New Orleans, little Eva becomes sickly with a wasting disease and her thoughts turn more and more toward winning soles for Jesus. She appeals to Topsy to be good. Topsy replies, "Could n't never be nothin' but [an African American], if I was ever so good. . . . If I could be skinned, and come white, I'd try then." Eva reassures Topsy, "People can love you, if you are black, Topsy. . . . Miss Ophelia would love you, if you were good." Topsy replies, "No; she can't bar me, 'cause I'm [an African American]! – she'd 's soon have a toad touch her!" Confronted with Topsy's feeling toward her, Miss Ophelia concurs, "I've always had a prejudice against [African Americans], and it's a fact, I never could bear to have that child touch me; but I did n't think she knew it. . . . I don't know how I can help it; they are disagreeable to me, – this child in particular, – how can I help feeling so?" Eva's health worsens and she calls everyone in the house to her sick room to witness to them about Jesus and to pass out snips of her golden hair as gifts by which they may remember her after she is gone. Afterward everyone leaves except Uncle Tom and her nanny, Mammy:

> 'Here, Uncle Tom,' said Eva, 'is a beautiful one for you. Oh, I am so happy, Uncle Tom, to think I shall see you in Heaven, for I'm sure I shall; and Mammy, – dear, good, kind, Mammy!' she said, fondly throwing her arms round her old nurse, – 'I know you'll be there, too.'"

A few days latter little Eva sinks toward death as her loved ones look on. Her father grips Uncle Tom's hand as, in anguish, he watches his daughter weaken. "Oh, Tom, my boy, it is killing me!" Tom looks heavenward and prays for a peaceful passing. Then he senses her struggle is over, "Oh, bless the Lord!, it's over, – it's over, dear Master! Look at her." Eva's father bends over her and whispers, "Oh, Eva, tell us what you see! What is it?" The child's last words are, "Oh! love, – joy, – peace!"

Augustine turns to Uncle Tom for religious guidance as he struggles with his grief. Augustine knows Christian teaching perhaps more completely than Tom, but seems unable to give himself to wholehearted faith in Jesus. Tom assures Augustine, "I's willin' to lay down my life, this blessed day, to see Mas'r a Christian." To this Augustine replies, "Poor foolish, boy! I'm not worth the love of one good, honest heart, like yours." Tom reassures, "Oh, Mas'r, dere's more than me loves you; the blessed Lord Jesus loves you." Augustine asks, "How do you know that, Tom?" To which Tom dispenses the wisdom of the ages: "Feels it in my soul. Oh, Mas'r! 'the love of Christ, that passeth knowledge.'" Some days later, Augustine tells Uncle Tom that he will soon make him independent and give him traveling money to return to Kentucky. He also writes out formal papers to make Topsy independent for Miss Ophelia, who has asked to soon take the child back with her to Vermont. It had taken a long time, but Miss Ophelia has finally opened her heart to the child and become comfortable hugging her and expressing motherly love toward her.

In a final debate over the rights and wrongs of African American bonding, Augustine asks Miss Ophelia, "suppose we should rise up tomorrow and [make all of them independent], who would educate these millions, and teach them how to use their [independence]?" Surmising that southern State people are too lazy for the task, Augustine says, "They will have to go [to the northern States], where labor is the fashion." Augustine then asks, "Is there enough Christian philanthropy, among your northern States, to bear with the process of their education and elevation? . . . How many families, in your town, would take in [an African American] man and woman, teach them, bear with them, and seek to make them Christian?" How many would take my butler "if I wanted to make him a clerk; or mechanics, if I wanted him taught a trade?" Speaking of many of his servants, Augustine explained that their European descent is as pure "as many a woman, north or south." Miss Ophelia replied, "Well, cousin, I know it is so." Recalling her personal learning process, Miss Ophelia projected, "I know there are many good people at the [northern States], who in this matter need only to be *taught* what their duty is, to do it."

That evening Augustine walks down to a cafe and is mortally wounded trying to break up a fight, which he accidentally encounters upon entering an establishment. He is carried back to the house. Pressing his hand to Tom's he cries out to his servant, "I am dying! Pray!" Augustine seems to accept Jesus as death nears: "It is coming home, at last! at last! at last!"

"They saw that the Mighty Hand was on him. Just before the spirit parted, he opened his eyes, with a sudden light, as of joy and recognition, and said 'Mother!' and then he was gone!"

In the aftermath of Augustine's unexpected death, his wife Marie decides to sell the house and all the staff except for her personal servant, and arranges to move to her parent's home. Although Marie is told that Augustine had promised to make Uncle Tom independent and pay his steamboat fare back to Kentucky, Marie refuses to honor the pledge. Tom is taken to the auction house.

A farmer named Simon Legree buys Tom. That day he also buys a young woman in her latter teens named Emmeline, but refuses to buy the girl's mother, who is distraught over the separation. Simon Legree is perhaps 40 to 50 years old. He had been born and raised in Massachusetts or a neighboring State. As a young man he had taken to the sea and later had spent considerable time on a pirate ship in the West Indies. A few years previously Legree had left the sea and purchased a remote farm on the Red River, in the same State of Louisiana, where he squeezed out a living raising cotton. Legree was notoriously cruel and inefficient. The once lovely farmhouse was in terrible condition. He had no wife or relatives on his place – just bonded African Americans, including two cruel foremen and a woman named Cassey, who took care of the house and his personal needs. There was no organization among the field workers, no cook, nothing. It was everyone for himself. Each worker was doled out a peck of dried corn. That was all each person was given to eat, and obviously contributed to poor health and eventual death. Tom arrived at the height of cotton picking. At the end of every long day in the field each worker was expected to wait in line for access to the hand-operated corn grinder, grind some corn, and prepare corn patties over a fire he or she would build. While on the riverboat, a stranger had asked Legree, "How long to they generally last?"

"Well, donno; 'cordin' as their constitution is. Stout fellers last six or seven years; trashy ones gets worked up in two or three. I used to, when I fust begun, have considerable trouble fussin' with 'em, and trying to make 'em hold out, – doctorin' on 'em up when they's sick, and givin' on 'em clothes and blankets, and what not, tryin' to keep 'em all sort o' decent and comfortable. Law, 't was n't no sort o' use; I lost money on 'em, and 't was heaps o' trouble. Now, you see, I just put 'em straight through, sick or well. When one [African American is] dead, I buy another; and I find it comes cheaper and easier, every way."

So for the first time in Harriet Stowe's book, Uncle Tom must work exceptionally hard. He picks cotton from dawn to dusk and weighs his production each night. He grinds his corn and cooks his supper of cornbread. He falls asleep in a crowded and dirty cabin. His only relaxation is time with his *Bible*, which he reads in snatches whenever he can. But it seems that Simon Legree wants to train Tom to be an overseer, and fears Tom is much too kind-hearted to handle the job. To test him, Legree commands Tom to beat a poor sick African American woman for alleged poor fieldwork. Tom refuses: "I never shall do it, – never!" Consequently, Legree figures he must beat Tom unmercifully to teach him meanness. Tom withstands the first beating, making no effort to fight back, and prays to God for strength as he suffers afterward. Cassey helps him recover a bit and helps him handle his fieldwork the next day. It seems Legree and Cassey had been fighting over household matters, and that had resulted in Cassey being banished temporarily to the fields.

Cassey is mostly of European descent and could be mistaken in a crowd for a full-blooded European. Cassey had known kindness and a Christian home in younger days. She and Tom talk of Legree's immense cruelty and she questions why God would let him rule over the place so unmercifully. Cassey tells Tom how her father had been a prosperous European American farmer and her mother had been a bonded African American of mostly European descent. When her father had died, she had been sold to a man who fell in love with her. She bore him children, and they were living happily though he had refused to make her independent and marry her. Then he had died of yellow fever and her children had been sold to the Simmons family in

New Orleans. She had been forced to work as a bonded prostitute as long as she had remained sufficiently attractive. After her clientele declined she had been sold to Simon Legree.

Uncle Tom recovers from the beating and assumes a cheerful outlook that aggravates Legree even more. Tom even sings hymns as he works. After many weeks all the cotton has been picked and Uncle Tom has more time to evangelize among his fellow workers. Then one night Cassey comes to Tom's cabin and whispers to him to come help her kill Legree, for she had worked him into a drunken stupor, but figures she is not strong enough to do the job herself. "No!" Tom replies. "I'd sooner chop my right hand off!" But Cassey has another idea. Legree is highly superstitious and Cassey figures she and Emmeline can pretend to run away, but double back and hide in the attic where Legree believes dreadful ghosts reside. After a few weeks Legree would give up searching the swamps and they could walk away to the riverboat landing without being followed. Cassey and Emmeline pull off the rouse without difficulty and hide unnoticed in the attic. But after a few days of searching Legree threatens to beat Uncle Tom until he tells what he knows about the women's flight. Tom says "I know, Mas'r; but I can't tell anything. I can die!"

"Mas'r, if you was sick, or in trouble, or dying, and I could save ye, I'd *give* ye my heart's blood; and, if taking every drop of blood in this poor old body would save your precious soul, I'd give 'em freely, as the Lord gave his for me. Oh, Mas'r! Don't bring this great sin on your soul! It will hurt you more than 't will me! Do the worst you can, my troubles 'll be over soon; but, if ye don't repent, yours won't *never* end!"

Simon Legree starts the beating and his two foremen, the bonded African Americans Sambo and Quimbo, finish the job. Later, as Tom lies near death on the ground Quimbo says, "Oh, Tom! we's been awful wicked to ye!" Tom murmurs, "I forgive ye, with all my heart!" Then Sambo pleads, "Oh Tom! do tell us who is Jesus, anyhow? Jesus, that's been a standin' by you so, all this night? – Who is he?" Quimbo and Sambo weep. Then Sambo confesses, "Why didn't I never hear this before? But I do believe! – I can't help it! Lord Jesus, have mercy on us!" Then Tom testifies, "Poor critturs! I'd be willin' to bar all I have, if it'll only bring ye to Christ! O Lord! Give me these two more souls, I pray!" And we are assured "That prayer was answered."

We are told that Uncle Tom's previous owners in Kentucky had been somewhat delayed in seeking out his whereabouts and helping to arrange his return to Kentucky. The head of the household, Mr. Shelby had died, and his son George, who, as a teenager, had loved Uncle Tom, had been delayed in traveling to New Orleans in search of him. Eventually George had made the trip, but it had taken many weeks to locate information on where Uncle Tom had been taken. Suddenly, as if by magic, George arrives at Legree's farm to find Uncle Tom near death just two days after the last horrible beating – lying unattended on the floor of a shed. "Oh Mas'r George, ye're too late. The Lord 's bought me, and is going to take me home, – and I long to go. Heaven is better than Kentuck." George Shelby cries out, "Oh don't die! It'll kill me! – it'll break my heart to think what you've suffered, – and lying in this old shed, here! Poor, poor fellow!" Tom gains enough strength to witness:

> "Don't call me poor fellow! I have been poor fellow; but that's all past and gone, now. I'm right in the door, going into glory! Oh, Mas'r George! Heaven has come! I've got the victory! – the Lord Jesus has given it to me! Glory be to his name!"

Tom dies a few moments later. Furious, George Shelby rises up and knocks Legree to the ground with one blow from his fist. Then he buries his friend and departs toward home.

Now Cassey and Emmeline are still in the attic protecting themselves with occasional ghostly noises and mysterious shadows. The pressure on Legree's soul becomes immense and he takes immediately to heavy drinking. In fact he drinks himself to death in a mere day or two. The night Legree dies, Cassey and Emmeline slip out unnoticed and make their way to the riverboat landing. They have plenty of traveling money, which they had taken from Legree. Cassey is dressed like a Creole Spanish lady and Emmeline pretends to be her servant. When they reach the riverboat landing, George Shelby is still there waiting for the next boat. So all board the same boat and head north up the Mississippi River.

During the voyage, we learn that a fellow passenger, a Madame de Thoux, is a sister to George Harris, the wife of Eliza and the father of little Harry, all three of whom had run away to Canada near the beginning of the story. Well, many years previously Madame de Thoux had been sold as a teenager. She explained to George Shelby, "I was bought by a good and generous man. He took me with him to the West Indies, [made me independent], and married me. It is but lately that he died; and I was coming up to Kentucky, to see if I could find and [purchase] my brother." George Shelby explains that George Harris was a fine man who married Eliza, a servant who had lived on his father's Kentucky farm. He explains the family now lives in Canada. Then we learn that George's deceased father had purchased Eliza, as a child, from the Simmons family in New Orleans. We now realize that Eliza must be Cassey's long-lost daughter.

So Madame de Thoux and Cassey travel to Montreal, Canada, and reunite with George, Eliza and their son Harry. The women take Emmeline with them. We learn George has become a successful machinist's helper. With Madame De Thoux's considerable money, the extended family journeys to France where George obtains a fine university education. During the voyage Emmeline falls in love with the ship's first mate, a full-blooded European, and the couple is married. Although he has far, far more European blood than African blood, George somehow identifies with sub-Sahara Africa and – surprise – he moves with his family from France to Liberia, which is on the west coast of Africa.

Meanwhile Ophelia has taken Topsy to Vermont and has provided for her education. Then Topsy leaves for some remote area of Africa to become a Christian missionary.

During this time George Shelby fills out papers in Kentucky, which make all of his bonded African Americans independent, but he does not turn them out on their own. They plead, "We don't want to be no freer than we are. We's allers had all we wanted. We don't want to leave de ole place, and Mas'r and Missis, and de rest!" George accommodates them all: "My good friends, there'll be no need for you to leave me. The place wants as many hands to work it as it did before." Then an old African American who had lived on the farm many years and is now blind lifts his voice toward the heavens: "Let us give thanks unto the Lord!"

Harriet Beecher Stowe's Concluding Remarks.

Harriet Beecher Stowe caps off her book with 10 pages of concluding remarks in which she recommends what northern States people should do about African American bonding in the southern States. She alleges that the events in her novel are "to a very great extent, authentic, occurring, many of them, either under her own observation or that of her personal friends." Yet Stowe submits a consolation: "The author hopes she has done justice to that nobility, generosity, and humanity, which in many cases characterize individuals in the [southern States]."

Stowe apparently does not understand that, on southern States farms, it was an economic necessity that African Americans be reasonably comfortable and happy and benefit from family ties. Nor did she understand that a supportive attitude was reinforced by the fact that European Americans and African Americans often grew up together, played as children together, worked together, hunted together, grew old together and died together. People were sold, but transfers did not dominate the scene, and young children mostly remained with their mothers. The most common age to move to another farm was the older teenage years when children approached adulthood.

Lamenting what she perceived to be a lack of effective anti-abuse law enforcement, Stowe concludes, "There is, actually, nothing to protect the [bonded African American's] life, but the *character* of the master." Stowe was referring to bonded African Americans, not to the persecuted Native Americans, when she wrote: "Nothing of tragedy can be written, can be spoken, can be conceived, that equals the frightful reality of scenes daily and hourly acting on our shores, beneath the shadow of American law, and the shadow of the cross of Christ." She asked her northern States readers, "Is this a thing for you to protect and countenance?"

Does Stowe encourage anyone to purchase, to rescue, a bonded African American, make him or her independent and train him or her to become self-sufficient? No! Stowe does not appeal to northern States people to rescue or give aid to southern States African Americans – she recommends they only stand in judgment. "But, what can any individual do? Of that, every individual can judge. There is one thing that every individual can do, – they can see to it that *they feel right*."

Then Stowe moves to the heart of the matter: how can northern States people exclude African Americans from their communities and help them at the same time? She asks: "Do you say: 'we don't want them here; let them go to Africa?'" Then she pronounces her recommendation. "Let the Church of the [northern

States] receive these poor sufferers in the spirit of Christ; receive them to the educating advantages of Christian republican society and schools, until they have attained to somewhat of a moral and intellectual maturity, and then assist them in their passage to those shores, where they may put in practice the lessons they have learned in America." So we realize that Stowe is not an Abolitionist, not even an Exclusionist — she is a **Deportationist**!

Then, as if forecasting the American Civil War, Harriet Beecher Stowe closes with dire warnings of the wrath of Almighty God, which will someday surely come. "For that day shall burn as an oven: and he shall appear as a swift witness against those that oppress the hireling in his wages, the widow and the fatherless, and that turn aside the stranger in his right: and he shall break in pieces the oppressor." How can the [Federation] of States be saved from disaster? Stowe closes with this warning:

> "Not by combining together, to protect injustice and cruelty, and making a common capital of sin, is this [Federation of sovereign States, known at the United States,] to be saved, — but by repentance, justice and mercy; for, not surer is the eternal law by which the millstone sinks in the ocean, than that stronger law by which injustice and cruelty shall bring on nations the wrath of Almighty God!"

Howard Ray White's Concluding Analysis of "Uncle Tom's Cabin."

So, we see that Harriet Beecher Stowe's novel, *Uncle Tom's Cabin*, neatly packaged 4 elements: the self-righteous mantle of Puritan Separatism and so-called "Abolitionism;" the all-European racial purity so dear to northern States Exclusionist propaganda; the sectional hatred so important to the future rise of the Republican Party, and the sinner's fate at the hand of Almighty God. None of her African American characters ever moved into the northern States to stay and live among Stowe's people. No compassionate sole from the northern States ever emerged in her story to pay money to make even one bonded person independent. It seems she fully subscribed to the wishful thinking that somehow all newly independent African Americans would be confined to the southern States, mostly as farm workers, or be deported to Africa, and that somehow they might willingly accept deportation to Africa, a land they had never personally known. Schoolteacher Stowe only advocated the addition of a few months of schooling and Christian education to prepare them for that Deportation journey.

Stowe even pandered to the revulsion she seemed to feel toward pureblooded Africans by mostly creating bonded characters that were so close to full-blooded Europeans that they could be mistaken for European Americans in a crowd. The only exceptions to this "almost white" cast of characters were Tom and Topsy. It appears that, in her heart of hearts, Harriet could partly, but with confidence, accept that pureblooded Africans benefited from bonding to a family of European descent, especially to a farming family, but she was simply horrified that a girl or a woman who looked more European than African could be bonded. She apparently believed featuring many such light-skinned characters in her novel added to its persuasiveness and taught newcomers from Central and Eastern Europe to fear that they too might someday be forced into bonded servitude, a status not unlike what many had recently fled Europe to escape.

Harriet Beecher Stowe's biographer, Noel Gerson, would later write of Harriet's much earlier trip to a Kentucky farm not far from a school where she had taught in Cincinnati, Ohio. An influential friend at the school had made the arrangements. It had been early fall 1833. Harriet had been 22 years old and not yet married. A friend, Mary Dutton, had accompanied her.

"The sheltered young ladies from [the northeastern States] had never seen a farm like it. The fields of corn, hemp, and tobacco were vast, and the blue grass of the lawns looked like a carpet. The house itself had broad verandas and large, high-ceilinged rooms that were sparsely but elegantly furnished with oversized mahogany pieces. Enormous coffee urns and teapots of silver gleamed everywhere."

"The young ladies were invited to join the [farm] owner and his family in what was described as a 'light repast,' which they privately thought was a banquet. There were large platters of cold chicken, duck, turkey, and ham. Potatoes and vegetables were heaped in bowls. Biscuits and cornbread were served hot, and there were more butter and cream on the table than the Beecher family used in a week. The servings were so lavish that expense obviously was no consideration. Harriet, who had spent her entire life in genteel poverty, later commented to Mary that such extravagance was sinful."

"The mistress of the house was a generous, warmhearted woman, and her husband, although inclined to drink large quantities of wine at the table, was a jovial man who was kind to his [bonded African Americans]. The [bonded African Americans] lived in vine-covered log cabins, each with its own small garden, and they seemed happy enough with their lot. From what the visitors could see, none was mistreated."

"One of the [bonded African Americans assigned to house work, who appeared to be of almost pure European descent], fascinated the [visitors]. She was a young woman of about their own age, stylishly attired in a snug-fitting dress. The visitors realized she was partly of [European American] ancestry, perhaps 75% [European American], and without question the descendant of a [European American] man and [an African American] woman. She was no less a [bonded person] because of her paternity, and the callousness of the system sickened the visitors."

Of that visit her friend Mary Dutton would write many years later:

"Hattie did not seem to notice anything in particular that happened, but sat much of the time as though abstracted in thought. When the [African Americans] did funny things and cut up capers, she did not seem to pay the slightest attention to them. Afterwards, however, in reading '*Uncle Tom*' I recognized scene after scene of that visit portrayed with the most minute fidelity, and knew at once where the material for that portion of the story had been gathered."

This concludes the summation of Harriet Stowe's historically powerful propaganda novel titled, "*Uncle Tom's Cabin*."

Of the torrent of newspaper, magazine and book-length propaganda, which poured forth from northern States printing presses in the 1850's, "*Uncle Tom's Cabin*" was recognized as the crowning achievement of the community of intellectuals that supported Abolitionism, Exclusionism, Deportationism and various blends of the three.

Deportationism was inbred in Harriet, for her father, Lyman Beecher, a famous Congregationalist and Calvinist minister, had, since her childhood, consistently supported the American Colonization movement, rationalizing that deportation to African would enable former American slaves to "carry to that country the Christianity of their [former] masters."

Four years after the publication of Harriet's novel, her brother, Henry Ward Beecher, famous as the Congregational minister at prosperous Plymouth Church in Brooklyn, New York, raised money for high-technology Springfield rifles to arm Exclusionist settlers departing from the northeastern States for political action in the new western territory known as "Bleeding Kansas." Arming such people with superior firepower was a widespread practice among financial supporters who were determined to defy Kansas Territory's legitimate Legislature by armed resistance, including terrorism. The result was "Bleeding Kansas," where a well-organized and rebellious Exclusionist shadow government justified terrorism by gangs such as the one led by the infamous John Brown and inspired the sectional political agitation throughout the northern States that made possible the rise of the Republican Party.

In her advancing years, living in retirement in Florida following the conquest of the Confederate States of America, Harriet Stowe's attitude toward people of African ancestry would change. Then, she would write that experiences of her later life had convinced her that the vast majority of African Americans, who were of little of no European descent, were not able to prosper as independent citizens to the extent she had envisioned them capable of at the time she was writing *Uncle Tom's Cabin.*

We must always remember that the Federal Invasion of the Confederacy (in violation of the Federal Constitution which then did not disallow State secession) killed 360,000 Federal invaders and 260,000 Confederate defenders. Thinking of those dead, what guidance should we acquire from our new understanding of *Uncle Tom's Cabin*?

I submit that we should take the following guidance: Each and every one of us must always beware of political agitators, for they often intend to deceive us for their own purposes. Present day political movements that are highly suspect of intentional deception and demagoguery include the Global Warming Scare, the socialistic concept of forced Wealth Redistribution and permissiveness toward Illegal Immigration. You can name many more.

How can we strive to avoid such dangerous demagoguery traps? Seek the truth! Yes, we must as individuals, by our own investigations, seek the truth — always. "Always seek the truth, for the truth shall set you free."

Understanding "The Battle Hymn of the Republic."

Introduction.

On November 19 a very important event took place in Washington City (Washington, D. C.), and it did not involve political leaders or military leaders. It involved Julia Ward Howe, age 41 years, the wife of Boston political activist Samuel Howe, who was a well known physician and caregiver of the blind, a former secret financial supporter of the nefarious terrorist leader John Brown and a long-time Abolitionist and Deportationist leader. That day, November 19, 1861, Julia wrote the lyrics to the Abolitionist crusade song, "*The Battle Hymn of the Republic.*"

You should know that Julia and Samuel Howe were not Christians as we think of Catholics, Baptists, Methodists, Presbyterians and so forth. During the 1850's and 1860's the Howe's were in lock-step with most Unitarians of the northeastern States of that era and thereby embraced a very free-thinking, Transcendentalist, pretend-Christian theology. As was customary with Unitarians in Massachusetts during that era, the Howe's belief in God and Jesus Christ (as we know it from the Christian *Bible*) was rather confused with Transcendentalism, Rationalism and The Doctrine of Necessity. Such confused religious belief was commonplace among Massachusetts intellectuals who had embraced the Republican Party.

A Picnic and the Glorification of John Brown.

It was from this background that Julia Ward Howe had been inspired to write the lyrics to her "*Battle Hymn of the Republic,*" the previous day, while picnicking with her husband and others as they watched a review of Massachusetts troops, just outside of Washington City. During the review she was captivated by Massachusetts soldiers singing "*John Brown's Body*" to a lovely tune that had been composed by South Carolinian William Steffe as a Methodist Sunday school and camp meeting song about 5 years earlier. But, it seems the review of troops was disturbed by some Confederate soldiers who opened fire on outlying pickets and sent the picnickers "scurrying back to the capital." It is appropriate to now examine in detail the evolution of and the meaning of "*The Battle Hymn of the Republic.*"

If you have read *Bloodstains*, Volume 2, *The Demagogues*, you will recall that Julia and Samuel Howe had known the terrorist leader John Brown personally; that Brown had visited them in their home in Boston; that Samuel had supported Brown with donations of money for the purchase of weapons and ammunition; that Samuel had fled for a while to Canada upon hearing news of Brown's capture at Harpers Ferry Armory; that Samuel had returned to Massachusetts only after he felt he was immune from imprisonment; that he had been forced to submit to questioning about his involvement before a special committee of the Federal Senate, and that he had lied under oath to the Senators to avoid being implicated in a plot of which he was a participant. Yes, Samuel Howe knew John Brown and he was a fellow conspirator who had given Brown encouragement and money. And his wife Julia, also a dedicated Abolitionist activist, had met Brown and admired him.

Howe was one of 6 prominent Abolitionist political activists who worked together to support John Brown. The others were Theodore Parker of Boston, the famous and very influential Unitarian leader; Gerit Smith of Peterboro, New York, a bachelor and heir to an immense fortune; Franklin Sanborn of Boston, a bachelor and Abolitionist who had become wealthy by marrying a dying woman; George Stearns of Boston, a wealthy lead-pipe manufacturer who supported Abolitionist causes, and Thomas Higginson of Massachusetts, a full-time Abolition political activist with an intense militant attitude. Their most important project had been raising money during the mid-1850's in support of terrorists from the northern States, including John Brown and his gang, who were going or had gone to Kansas Territory to drive out settlers from the southern States.

When news arrived of the October 16, 1859 raid on Harpers Ferry Armory by Brown's gang, like Howe, Franklin Sandborn and George Stearns fled to Canada for a while — Theodore Parker, who was very ill at the time over in Italy, hoping to recover, wrote letters praising John Brown's attack and soon thereafter died — and Gerit Smith became sick with fear and had himself committed to an insane asylum to avoid being implicated. These were the wealthy and influential supporters of John Brown's earlier terrorist attacks in Kansas Territory and his last attack, that being against the Harpers Ferry Armory. And Julia Ward Howe was of the same persuasion and supportive of the efforts of her husband and the other 5 men, although she probably did not know the extent to which they were funding terrorist murderers.

Transforming "Say, Brothers" into a Song of Hatred.

Now I turn to William Steffe's song, "*Say, Brothers,*" which Julia Ward Howe appropriated for her "*Battle Hymn.*" William Steffe had composed "*Say, Brothers*" about 1856 (some sources say 1853). He was a South Carolinian (some sources say a Virginian, some say a Georgian). The tune and lyrics were easy to sing and harmonize and were influenced by African American music and folk music traditions. A leader could easily teach the words to a group of singers as they all sang along. The "*Say, Brothers*" song had become popular at religious revivals (also called camp meetings) and Sunday schools, both among European Americans and African Americans. It seemed to have first become popular around Charleston, South Carolina. Later, the song had made its way north and had been picked up by Federal army soldiers, who had changed the words, except for the refrain, to transform the song into one praising John Brown.

Generally speaking, "*Say, Brothers*" was sung while inviting folks to join the church at the conclusion of a revival meeting.

Verse 1:

"Say, brothers, will you meet us,
Say, brothers, will you meet us,
Say, brothers, will you meet us
    On Canaan's happy shore?"

Refrain:

"Glory, glory hallelujah,
Glory, glory hallelujah,
Glory, glory hallelujah,
    For ever, ever-more!"

Verse 2:

"By the grace of God we'll meet you,
By the grace of God we'll meet you,
By the grace of God we'll meet you,
    Where parting is no more."

Verse 3:

"Jesus lives and reigns forever,
Jesus lives and reigns forever,
Jesus lives and reigns forever,
 On Canaan's happy shore."

We see that the above was a pure Christian song of invitation. The hymn is about coming together by the grace of God — believers coming together with loved ones and with Jesus after passing on. It's about brotherly love. It's about gladness and happiness. It truly aims to glorify God in accordance with the teachings of Jesus Christ. "Glory glory, hallelujah!" It sure seems to fit.

"John Brown's Body," Praise of a Terrorist Leader.

Well, in 1861, two years after the conviction and execution of terrorist John Brown, certain Federal soldiers, who were imbued with an enthusiasm for Abolitionism, a hatred of southern States people and an admiration of Brown, adapted for their militant purposes the *"Say, Brothers"* hymn, resulting is a gory hymn praising their hero. The tune was the same and the "Glory, glory hallelujah!" was the same, but the meaning was in no way an expression of Christianity. This is the John Brown song:

Verse 1:

"John Brown's body lies a mould'ring in the grave.
John Brown's body lies a mould'ring in the grave.
John Brown's body lies a mould'ring in the grave.
 His soul is marching on!"

The chorus:

"Glory, glory hallelujah!
Glory, glory hallelujah!
Glory, glory hallelujah!
 His soul is marching on!"

Remaining verses:

"The stars of Heaven are looking kindly down.
The stars of Heaven are looking kindly down.
The stars of Heaven are looking kindly down.
 On the grave of old John Brown!

28

"He's gone to be a soldier in the army of the Lord.
He's gone to be a soldier in the army of the Lord.
He's gone to be a soldier in the army of the Lord.
 His soul is marching on!

"John Brown's knapsack is strapped upon his back.
John Brown's knapsack is strapped upon his back.
John Brown's knapsack is strapped upon his back.
 His soul is marching on!

"His pet lambs will meet him on the way.
His pet lambs will meet him on the way.
His pet lambs will meet him on the way.
 And they'll go marching on!

"They will hang Jeff Davis on a sour apple tree.
They will hang Jeff Davis on a sour apple tree.
They will hang Jeff Davis on a sour apple tree.
 As they go marching on!"

Like "*Say, Brothers*", the song glorifying the terrorist, John Brown, is easily taught by a song leader and easily past along by oral tradition. It expresses the Unitarianism of the time, with a touch of Christianity, as it elevates John Brown to a militant angel who is admired by "the stars," serves as a soldier in the "army of the Lord," returns in spirit form to lead the Federal soldiers, called his "pet lambs," as they push southward in their invasion of Maryland, Kentucky and Missouri and, that accomplished, on into the Confederacy, climaxing with the hanging of President Jeff Davis. We are struck by the free-thinking 1860's Unitarian mind that makes "stars" into holy beings, glibly transforms a convicted and executed leader of terrorists and murderers like John Brown into a glorious angel, and advances that angel as the leader of Federal invasion forces. We also observe that the song is not critical of the seceded States or the bonding of African Americans; that criticism seems to be taken for granite.

"The Battle Hymn of the Republic," as First Written.

This was the "John Brown" song Julia Ward Howe heard Federal soldiers singing as she, her husband and other picnickers watched a review of Federal troops just outside of Washington City on November 18, 1861; that is before they were disturbed by some Confederate soldiers who opened fire on outlying pickets and sent the picnickers "scurrying back to the capital." She liked the tune and probably did not know its origin — probably did not know that a man from the southern States had written it — did not know that the lovely tune had been composed by South Carolinian William Steffe as a Methodist Sunday school and camp meeting song about 5 years earlier. It seemed to her that Massachusetts soldiers singing the John Brown song symbolized "the glory of the coming of the Lord."

Although she felt the meaning was tremendous, she felt the lyrics were trite and insufficiently inspiring. So that night and the next morning, at Willards Hotel in Washington City, she wrote the first version of a new set of lyrics which also drew upon the emotions surrounding John Brown's martyrdom. She titled her set of replacement lyrics, *The Battle Hymn of the Republic*." Here is the "*Battle Hymn*" as she first wrote it. Notice how she opens in the first person, witnessing to others about how those Massachusetts troops singing John Brown's "soul is marching on" had inspired her to believe she had "seen the glory of the coming of the Lord."

Verse 1:
"Mine eyes have seen the glory of the coming of the Lord.
He is trampling out the <u>wine press,</u> where the grapes of wrath are stored,
He hath loosed the fateful <u>lightnings of his</u> terrible swift sword,
His truth is marching on.

The chorus:
"Glory, glory hallelujah!
Glory, glory, hallelujah!
Glory, glory, hallelujah!
His truth is marching on."

Remaining verses:
"I have seen <u>him</u> in the watchfires of a hundred circling camps.
They have builded <u>him</u> an altar in the evening dews and damps,
I can read his righteous sentence by the dim and flaring lamps,
His day is marching on.

"I have read a <u>burning Gospel</u> writ in <u>fiery</u> rows of steel,
As ye deal with my contemners, so with you my grace shall deal,
Let the <u>hero, born of woman,</u> crush the serpent with his heel,
<u>Our</u> God is marching on.

"He has sounded out the trumpet that shall never call retreat,

30

He has waked the earth's dull sorrow with a high ecstatic beat,
Oh! Be swift my soul to answer him, be jubilant my feet!
    Our God is marching on.

"In the whiteness of the lilies he was born across the sea,
With a glory in **his** bosom that shines out on you and me,
As **he** died to make men holy, let us die to make men free,
    Our God is marching on.

"He is coming like the glory of the morning on the wave,
He is widom to the mighty, he is succour to the brave,
So the world shall be his footstool, and the soul of Time his slave,
    Our God is marching on."

"The Battle Hymn of the Republic," as Published.

This version of Julia Ward Howe's Lyrics was passed among some friends. Publication was arranged for the February 1, 1862 issue of The Atlantic Monthly magazine, on the front cover, no less. Before publication, Howe and others modified the words a bit. The published version became the official set of lyrics. Note that I have underlined in both sets of lyrics those words that differ. Here is the "Battle Hymn" as it was published.

Verse 1:
    "Mine eyes have seen the glory of the coming of the Lord:
    He is trampling out the vintage where the grapes of wrath are stored;
    He hath loosed the fateful lightning of His terrible swift sword:
        His truth is marching on.

The Chorus:
    "Glory, glory hallelujah!
    Glory, glory, hallelujah!
    Glory, glory, hallelujah!
        His truth is marching on."

Remaining verses:
    "I have seen Him in the watch-fires of a hundred circling camps,
    They have builded Him an altar in the evening dews and damps;
    I can read His righteous sentence by the dim and flaring lamps:
        His day is marching on.

"I have read a fiery gospel writ in burnished rows of steel:
"As ye deal with my contemners, so with you my grace shall deal;

31

Let the <u>Hero, born of woman,</u> crush the serpent with his heel,
  <u>Since</u> God is marching on.

"He has sounded forth the trumpet that shall never call retreat;
<u>He is sifting out the hearts of men before His judgment-seat:</u>
Oh, be swift, my soul, to answer <u>Him!</u> be jubilant, my feet!
  <u>Our</u> God is marching on.

"In the <u>beauty</u> of the lilies <u>Christ</u> was born across the sea,
With a glory in **his** bosom that <u>transfigures</u> you and me:
As **he** died to make men holy, let us die to make men free,
  While God is marching on."

At this time, it is appropriate to examine in detail the evolution of and the meaning of "*The Battle Hymn of the Republic*."

The Howe's and most of their friends were Unitarians and thereby embraced its free-thinking pretend-Christian theology. As was customary with Unitarians, the Howe's belief in God and Jesus Christ as presented in the Christian Bible was rather confused with Transcendentalism, Rationalism and The Doctrine of Necessity. Such confused religious belief was commonplace among intellectuals who embraced the Republican Party. We need to understand this as we examine the lyrics. We also need to understand the remarkable extent to which Unitarians and northern States Christian leaders — from the northeastern States westward along the Great Lakes — glorified John Brown after his gang's rather foolish terrorist attack at the Harpers Ferry Armory in northern Virginia — made him into a heroic martyr — even likened him to Jesus Christ. You may want to review that history as told in my epic history from which this booklet is drawn: *Bloodstains*, Volume 2, *The Demagogues*.

Understanding What "The Battle Hymn" is Saying.

The words of the **first verse** appear to have been inspired by hearing the John Brown song the previous day, especially the third verse: "He's gone to be a soldier in the army of the Lord." It was there, the previous day, that "Mine eyes" — that is "Julia Ward Howe's eyes" — saw the "glory." And it is easy to believe that it is the martyrdom of John Brown that is "trampling out the wine press" and attacking with "his terrible swift sword" — that John Brown's "truth is marching on." You see, the "his" is not capitalized. But, in the edited version of "*The Battle Hymn*," published in February 1862, "his" is changed to "His" to switch the meaning from John Brown's "terrible swift sword" to God's "terrible swift sword." Since "His" begins the last line of the verse, we cannot tell if she is talking about God's "truth" or John Brown's "truth," but it is not hard to assume she means John Brown's "truth."

The words of the **second verse** readily suggest that Julia Ward Howe — she is in first person, she is the "I" — sees John Brown in the "hundred circling camps" and sees soldier's building "an altar" to John Brown or to his alleged "spirit" — this being evident by the use of a lower-case "him" instead of a capitalized "Him." Again, in line three, she uses a lower case "him" to specify that the "righteous sentence" of death to Confederates is seen as being handed down by the spirit of John Brown. But John Brown's presence would become obscured from verse 2 before publication in February, as the "him" would be replaced with "Him." Yet can anyone doubt that "His day" is John Brown's day, that John Brown's "day is marching on?"

The words of the **third verse** suggest that Julia Ward Howe — again she is in first person, she is the "I" — has read the letters and proclamations of John Brown and is equating them to a "fiery gospel," and seeing them written in "fiery" or "burnished rows of steel," which reminds us of the 1,000 steel-tipped wooden spears that John Brown's small gang had on hand during his terrorist attack on Harper's Ferry Armory. The second line mentions "my contemners." A "contemner" is a despiser and a scorner, who treats his adversary as if he is mean and despicable. So, the second line means this: "As ye (Federal soldiers) deal with my contemners (Confederate defenders), so with you (Federal soldiers) my (John Brown's) grace shall deal." You see, I find no evidence that she is invoking God's Grace; she must be invoking a grace dispensed by John Brown's spirit. Notice that nothing in that line was changed in the edit for publication. In the third line, "hero born of woman," seems to mean John Brown, the hero, and "serpent" seems to mean the Confederacy and the practice of bonding African Americans. Of course, the Devil is often called the "serpent" in the Bible, but I do not see the Devil being invoked in this set of lyrics. We are also tempted to see John Brown in the third line because he would be removed from it during the edit prior to publication. The line would be changed to "Let the Hero, born of woman," — the capitalization of hero serves to transfer the meaning from John Brown to Jesus Christ. Then the verse closes with, "Our God is marching on." Perhaps it is Howe's Unitarian thinking that claims "Our God" is different from the God to which many

Confederates prayed. Prior to publication, "Our God" was changed to "Since God," to complement the capitalization of "hero." So we see in the third verse that there was clearly an initial attempt to glorify, even deify, John Brown, and that this was abandoned before publication.

John Brown is clearly the mover and shaker in the **fourth verse**. Surely it was John Brown who "Sounded out the trumpet that shall never call retreat" and "has waked the earth's dull sorrow with a high ecstatic beat." Julia Ward Howe is crediting John Brown with starting the crusade that she sees unfolding before her eyes — the holy military crusade aimed southward. She equates the political and personal sins of southern States society to "earth's dull sorrow" and John Brown's assault upon it as "a high ecstatic beat." Ecstatic is derived from ecstasy — pertaining to or resulting from ecstasy, being delightful beyond measure. Then Howe admonishes herself, and singers of the lyrics as well, to "be swift . . . to answer him," that is, "be swift . . . to answer John Brown's call to battle; and be "jubilant" over the opportunity to so crusade. She closes with reference again to "Our God" inferring that the people of the southern States have some other God. But this obvious calling to follow John Brown to battle would be seriously edited before Howe's lyrics would be published in February. The second line would be completely rewritten to become, "He is sifting out the hearts of men before His judgment-seat," and in the third line "him" would become "Him," thereby removing John Brown and suggesting that God or Jesus Christ is "sifting out the hearts" and sitting in "His judgment-seat."

As originally written, the **fifth verse** continues the deification of John Brown. "In the whiteness of the lilies he was born across the sea," paints an image of a Christ-like John Brown being carried across a vast span, such as being carried from earth to Heaven. The reference is not to Christ because the "he" is not capitalized. "Born," also sometimes spelled "Borne," is the past participle of "bear" and has potentially far more meanings than giving birth to a baby. Anyway, what is the point of mentioning that Jesus Christ was born in Bethlehem, beyond the far shore of the Atlantic Ocean? Furthermore, John Brown is pictured as being carried from earth to Heaven, "With a glory in his bosom that shines out on you and me." Clearly the terrorist leader is being carried to Heaven by angels, his soul being filled with a "glory" that shines its light down upon the people of the northern States, like a bright star, offering encouragement that they join his spirit in the holy crusade. Equating John Brown to Jesus Christ reaches a crescendo in the third line, where Howe had written, "As he died to make men holy, let us die to make men free." Again we see "he" not "He." Anyway, Jesus Christ did not die to make bonded people independent, he died for their sins, and other people's sins, to symbolize God's grace. Again the God that is seen "marching on" is "Our God," somehow different from other people's God. But before this verse would be published in February, the meaning would be inverted: Jesus Christ would replace John Brown. The wording would then seem strange and forced as it would become, "In the beauty of the lilies Christ was born across the sea, with a glory in his bosom that transfigures you and me." This message now strikes me as silly and without pertinence. But did the editors also goof and overlook two capitalizations? Why did they not capitalize "his bosom?" and "he died?" Perhaps that was an oversight.

The **sixth verse** would not be published in February 1862. It would be discarded for good. It can be read with the "he" representing John Brown or Jesus Christ or God. In any event it speaks of an awesome power in support of the Federal armies. I do not know what is meant by "the soul of Time is his slave," Whose slave? Why is "Time" capitalized? In any event it is apparent that Julia Ward Howe was determined to end her lyrics with the word "slave." And that she did. But, alas, the editing process would strike out the sixth verse entirely. That verse would not be published in February.

We see that Julia Ward Howe's intent was to write a variation of the John Brown song she had heard the day before, but with a much more literary and glorious message — one that would be too complex to pass along orally in sing-alongs, but one that would be enduring in published form and advance the moral cause of the crusade she saw gaining momentum.

But what of the meaning? Whether the lyrics glorify John Brown or glorify Jesus Christ, the allegation is clearly that God — "Our God" — the God of the northern States — is in lock-step with the Federal army as it fights to subjugate Maryland, Kentucky and Missouri and then march on southward to conquer the seceded States of the Confederacy. It clearly condemns the people of those States as being sinful and deserving of the wrath of God. It clearly adorns the Federal Army with the holy task of inflicting God's wrath upon its intended victim. It clearly advocates a holy crusade against the infidels.

This brings me to a conclusion that I wish to share with you. Here's a question for you: In our-present day representative democracy why must the descendents of subjugated Maryland, Kentucky and Missouri and the descendents of the Confederate States suffer through the *"Battle Hymn of the Republic"* on patriotic occasions? This is a song that justifies the killing of 360,000 Federals and glorifies the killing of 260,000 Confederates, that being required to consummate the conquest of the southern States, to conquer a people who only wanted to be left alone to govern themselves, a right the Federal Constitution had, at that time, granted to each State. This is a song that glorifies the military conquest of one-half of the States by the people of the other half — a war that escalated into a scorched earth policy where Federals destroyed farms and livestock, laying waste to the southern economy and the southern landscape. This is a song about a political Civil War between Republicans and Democrats. This is not a song that honors the defeat of an invading army. Far from it! It is a song praising and urging on that invading army.

Why Not Sing "Say, Brothers" Instead?

If we Americans today wish to ease the pain and suffering of that history, we ought not to be pouring salt into the old wounds! Performances of *"The Battle Hymn of the Republic"* ought to be banned as unfit for a nation that seeks a united citizenry. The lyrics and tune of *"Say, Brothers"*, attributed to William Steffe of South Carolina, is wonderful. If folks want to sing that lovely tune, especially in full chorus when it is the most magnificent, then encourage them sing instead with those old words of brotherly love — encourage them to sing:

> "Say brothers, will you meet us?
> Say brothers, will you meet us?
> Say brothers, will you meet us?
>   On Canaan's happy shore."

> "Glory, glory hallelujah!
> Glory, glory hallelujah!
> Glory, glory hallelujah!
>   For ever, ever more!"

That's a song about coming together, about happiness. I prefer to sing songs about coming together, about happiness. There is enough hatred and killing in this world — past and present — without glorifying it in song.

SAY, BROTHERS.

1. Say, brothers, will you meet us, Say, brothers, will you meet us,
Ref.— Glory, glo-ry, hal-le - lu - jah, Glory, glo-ry, hal-le - lu - jah,

Say, broth-ers, will you meet us, On Ca - naan's hap-py shore?
Glo - ry, glo - ry, hal - le - lu - jah, For ev - er, ev - er - more!

Verse 2

By the grace of God we'll meet you,
By the grace of God we'll meet you,
By the grace of God we'll meet you,
Where parting is no more.

Verse 3

Jesus lives and reigns forever,
Jesus lives and reigns forever,
Jesus lives and reigns forever,
On Canaan's happy shore.

And Why Not Sing "Dixie," Too?

Unlike the "*Battle Hymn*," "*Dixie*," the most popular song among defenders of the Confederacy, is a happy song about home. Yet, "*Dixie*" is today effectively banned from public performance while "*The Battle Hymn of the Republic*" is embraced as supposedly wholesome, uplifting and patriotic.

Here are the lyrics to "*Dixie*" without the original minstrel dialect.

"Oh, I wish I was in the land of cotton;
Old times there are not forgotten.
Look away! Look away!
Look away! Dixie Land.

"In Dixie Land where I was born,
Early on one frosty morn.
Look away! Look away!
Look away! Dixie Land.

"Oh, I wish I was in Dixie!
Hooray! Hooray!
In Dixie Land I'll take my stand
To live and die in Dixie.
Away! Away!
Away down south! In Dixie!

Frankly, as a nation today, we ought to be proudly singing "*Dixie*" as a regional song and reverently singing "*Say, Brothers*" as a national song, while we relegate "*The Battle Hymn of the Republic*" to historical libraries and museums to be occasionally sung to students who are trying to understand how civil wars get started and get sustained.

Dixie

Daniel D Emmett/ Arr. Criswell

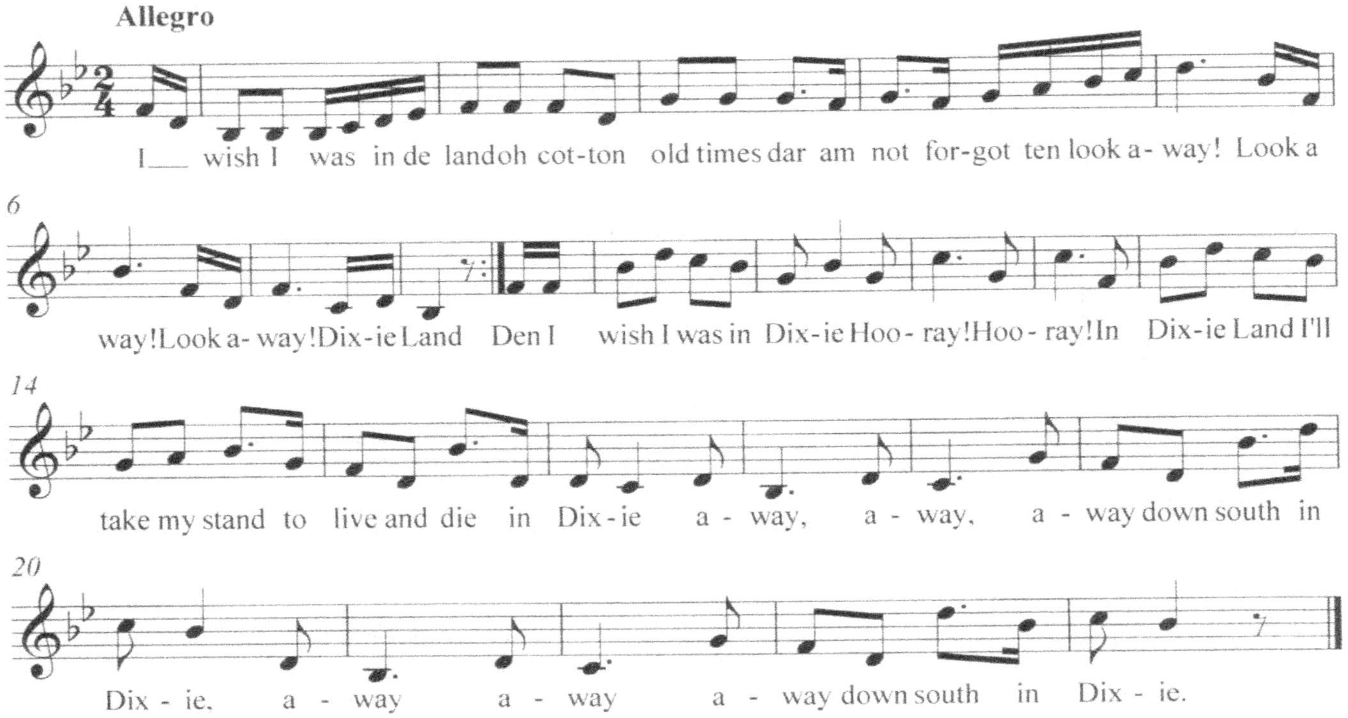

Concluding Remarks.

Of this I have said enough. I am through. I can only hope my essay on these songs has helped you sort out the issues related to them, the attitudes that caused and sustained the War Between the States and the trouble we have today in teaching its truthful history.

We must always remember that the Federal Invasion of the Confederacy (in violation of the Federal Constitution which then did not disallow State secession) killed 360,000 Federal invaders and 260,000 Confederate defenders. Thinking of those dead, what guidance should we acquire from our new understanding of *"Say, Brothers," "John Brown's Body"* and *"The Battle Hymn of the Republic?"*

I submit that we should take the following guidance:

> Each and every one of us must always beware of political agitators, for they often intend to deceive us for their own purposes. Present day political movements that employ deception and demagoguery include the Global Warming Scare, the socialistic concept of forced Wealth Redistribution, Ever-expanding the Federal Government and our Federal Debt, and Permissiveness toward Illegal Immigration. You can name many more.

> How can we strive to see through such dangerous demagoguery traps? Seek the truth! Yes, we must as individuals, by our own investigations, seek the truth — always. "Always seek the truth, for the truth shall set you free."

References for Both Essays.

References for "*Understanding 'Uncle Tom's Cabin'*:"

Uncle Tom's Cabin, or Life Among the Lowly, Harriet Beecher Stowe, many publishers, 1852.

Reminiscences 1819-1899, Howe Julia Ward, 1899, Reprinted in 1969 by Negro University Press, New York, pages 244-280.

Bloodstains, An Epic History of the Politics that Produced and Sustained the American Civil War and the Political Reconstruction that Followed, Volume 2, *The Demagogues*, Howard Ray White, Amazon.com or through author direct.

References for "*Understanding 'The Battle Hymn of the Republic'*:"

"*Say, Brothers,*" Steffe, William, 1853 or 1856, South Carolina Camp Meeting Song of Invitation, later published in Hymn and Tune Book of The Methodist Episcopal Church South, Nashville, Tennessee, 1889.

The Secret Six, John Brown and the Abolitionist Movement, Otto Scott, Uncommon Books, Murphy, CA, 1979.

"*John Brown's Body Lies a Mould'ring in the Grave*", authors of lyrics is unknown, a Federal army inspirational song originating near The Great Lakes in 1861, the music and refrain, written by William Steffe, originated earlier in South Carolina.

"*The Battle Hymn of the Republic,*" Howe, Julia Ward, a poem printed in *The Atlantic Monthly*, February 1862, the music and refrain, added later, written by William Steffe, originated earlier in South Carolina.

"*Dixie*" (also called "*Dixie-Land*" and "*I Wish I Was in Dixie-Land*"), Daniel D. Emmett, 1859.

Bloodstains, An Epic History of the Politics that Produced and Sustained the American Civil War and the Political Reconstruction that Followed, Volume 3, *The Bleeding*, Howard Ray White, Amazon.com or through author direct.

Author's Goodbye.

Thank you for reading the history concerning *Uncle Tom's Cabin* and *The Battle Hymn of the Republic* — a history concerning two very influential women whose respective literary work contributed so much to a horrific, yet unnecessary, war between the American states, shattering the normal bonds of brotherly love, bonds torn asunder by the mighty tugs of political and commercial ambition. Want to learn more? Call me at 704-846-4411 or 704-242-0022 so we can talk. I always try to take time to discuss history with my readers.

Howard Ray White

P. S.

Let us sing, sisters;

Let us sing brothers;

Let us sing: *"Say, Brothers,"*

And embrace,

And dream of glorious days

On Canaan's happy shore.

The End.